It's Raining Wisdom

The Golden Nuggets of God

Sandra L. Ross

Copyright © 2019 by Sandra L. Ross

All rights reserved. No part of this publication may be reproduced by any means, graphics, electronic, or mechanical, including photocopying, recording, taping, or by any information storage retrieval system without the written permission of the publisher except in the case of brief quotations embodied in critical articles and reviews.

Sandra L. Ross/Rejoice Essential Publishing
PO BOX 512
Effingham, SC 29541

www.republishing.org

Unless otherwise indicated, scripture is taken from the King James Version.

It's Raining Wisdom/ Sandra L. Ross

ISBN-13: 978-1-952312-41-0

Library of Congress Control Number: 2020920881

Dedication

Jesus, thank You for being my biggest cheerleader and for never giving up on me. Thank you that today I am in my blessed place and I see it now.

Thank you to my family and friends.

Thank you to my covenant sister. You loved me during the good, bad, and ugly seasons of my life. Thank you for covering me in prayers, your honesty, and prophetic insight. God Wink, you know who you are.

Thank you to my 7th-grade teacher, Mrs. Noble. You told me that you would not be surprised if you opened up a book one day and saw my name as the author. Your words inspired me, and your words carried weight. I never forgot what you said and today they are manifested. Words spoken in season can change a life forever.

Acknowledgment

I want to thank Prophetess Kimberley Moses, a prolific writer for the kingdom of God. You inspire me in so many ways and my life has tremendously been blessed. Your writer's workshop encouraged me to pick up my pen and write, thus finishing my first book. Thank you for being so generous with what God has given you and imparting into the lives of others. I thank Rejoice Essential Publishing for your spirit of excellence, your time and talents in bringing this book into fruition.

Contents

ACKNOWLEDGMENT..........................ix

CHAPTER 1:   Revelation of Golden Nuggets............................1

CHAPTER 2:   God Given Faith................4

CHAPTER 3:   The Pitfalls of Fear........12

CHAPTER 4:   God's Promises...............18

CHAPTER 5:   Single............................24

CHAPTER 6:   Overcoming Challenges of the Heart.....................31

CHAPTER 7:   God's Comfort................39

CHAPTER 8:   The Result (Process, Promotion, Testimony and Destiny)..........................45

ABOUT THE AUTHOR......................60

REFERENCES 62

CHAPTER 1

Revelation of Golden Nuggets

In 2015, I had a vision of the Lord and saw the following:

I looked up into the sky and the heavens opened. The sky turned the most heavenly blue. Then I saw a big window open with four windowpanes, which allowed the bright sun to shine through. Also, there was a wave of water like a tidal coming in through the window. It was raining like a flood flash and it was still so bright. Surprisingly, it was down pouring golden coins that were stamped Jesus on one side and on the other side Wisdom. The coins had ridges just like real money.

The Lord told me to buy a journal and write down all the golden coins He imparted into me because it will be the first book I write. A book that will give wisdom, hope, and healing to those lacking faith, gripped by fear, or dealing with heart issues. Also, it will help you to not give up in Christ.

I call these heavenly deposits, golden coins, or Golden Nuggets of wisdom, which some of these were given to me during various phases of my faith walk as a young Christian. These nuggets encouraged and strengthened me to keep pressing in God not to give up.

Each chapter represents a season in my Christian journey and has golden nuggets that the Lord ministered, comforted, and healed me. What are golden nuggets? I will explain as given to me by the Lord. Golden nuggets are God's spoken words and the Holy Ghost digging deep and revealing His hidden treasures and promises.

In my Christian walk, faith and fear was a biggie for me. How can I have faith in what I could not see and too afraid to trust? Because of the Father's love, mercy, and golden nuggets deposits, I was able to walk it out in Jesus.

It is my prayer that these golden nuggets will comfort and minister to every reader as I was. I pray in the name of Jesus that the windows of heaven would open concerning you. I pray for a down pouring of the Holy Ghost and that you be downloaded with heavenly deposits of encouragement, strength, and faith.

CHAPTER 2

God Given Faith

Faith[1] **(noun)-**

Complete trust or confidence in something or someone, a strong belief in God, belief without evidence.

Synonyms:

---

1. Merriam-Webster.com Dictionary, s.v. "faith," accessed September 9, 2020, https://www.merriam-webster.com/dictionary/faith.

Trust, confidence, belief, conviction

Scripture:

Hebrews 11:1 says, "Now faith is the substance of things hoped for, the evidence of things not seen."

As a babe in Christ, I struggled with faith. I was in the Navy stationed in California. I read the story of Gideon (Judges 6) and I heard testimonies of laying a fleece before the Lord. I needed direction about a situation, so I asked God, "If this is your will, then show me butterflies. Not just any kind, but let them be monarch butterflies." The next day, I picked up a newspaper and on the front page was a picture of monarch butterflies. Also, I was working on the flight line and a beautiful monarch butterfly flew right next to me. That whole day I kept seeing butterflies and people were talking to me about them. WOW!! This encouraged me and I would lay the fleece before the Lord all the time. Each time He would show Himself to me, my faith would increase.

After a while, laying a fleece before the Lord was no longer my go-to.

Throughout my walk in Christ, I saw and lived the impossible in God. He made ways when there seemed to be no way. I recently got out the Navy and money was tight. I heard the Lord say, "Go and open your door." I opened the door and a twenty-dollar bill blew and landed at my foot. You may ask, "So what's the big deal?" Well, a miracle occurred because of how the door is positioned in my apartment, there is no reasonable explanation as to how the wind was able to blow money in my direction. It was God. Have faith in Him.

Golden Nuggets

I'm not discouraged by what I see, but I'm encouraged by what I don't see because I walk by faith and not by sight.

Faith without works is like a debit card never activated. It's useless and dead.

Exercise your faith like an ATM card. The more you use it, the more points you get. Exercise your faith and watch it grow.

Faith in action produces a reaction.

Faith withdrawn or used is like making a deposit in your savings account. Your faith will increase.

Favor is nothing without faith.

God got this.

Dreaming about faith is doing nothing. You're idle.

I trust God. How about you?

I agree with the Word of God. I believe it and I walk in it.

Where there's faith, you'll find favor.

Favor is faith activated.

Unbelief is likened to paralysis. You're not moving. There is no action. You're just stuck. Faith without works is dead.

Faith kick starts favor.

When stepping or walking out in faith, look up at the hills and not down at your situation.

Serve God without borders. Expect the impossible.

Don't put God in a box. He's the God of the unexpected and the unexplainable. Ask Sarah and Abraham.

Faith is invisible till it's acted upon, then it's visible.

Faith is likened to a bodybuilder that exercises their muscles until they become bigger. The more you exercise your faith, the greater it is. This kind of faith moves mountains and heals the sick.

Got faith? Then you have God's attention.

Mountains are moved in response to faith spoken.

Move God...have faith.

No Faith. God's Not Moved.

Faith causes a God response.

Please God. Have faith.

No faith. GOD's not moved.

The command (spoken word) is faith in action.

I believe. I have faith.

Words spoken in faith carries weight. It causes change.

Faith is a sound that gets God's attention.

Faith is just like a muscle and if it's not used, it will shrink.

Our faith ministers to God. He loves when we trust and believe in Him.

GOD said, "I see everything and I know everything before you do. How can you not have faith in me?"

Faith is the catalyst for transition/change.

God tends to every plant and animal. And yes, even the insects. Why wouldn't He tend to you?

All your needs I knew and have made provision. Only believe in me, your provider.

Expect your miracle. Look for it.

No faith. No God response.

Move God. Have faith.

Mountains move in response to faith in action, spoken.

The commanded word is faith activated.

Words spoken in faith carries authority. It causes things to change/shift.

God spoke faith to the void and order took place.

Faith is a sound that causes a shaking and produces change.

I believe. Therefore, I have faith.

CHAPTER 3

The Pitfalls of Fear

Fear² (noun)

An unpleasant, often strong emotion caused by expectation or awareness of danger. A concern of what may happen, worry.

Synonyms:

---

2. Merriam-Webster.com Dictionary, s.v. "fear," accessed September 9, 2020, https://www.merriam-webster.com/dictionary/fear.

Terror, loss of courage, anxiety, dread.

Scripture:

2 Timothy 1:7 says, "For God hath not given us the spirit of fear; but of power, and of love, and of a sound mind".

The spirit of fear was like a school yard bully with a host of other comrades (spirts). I was so afraid of everything: relationships, intimacy, people and their opinions, failing, and succeeding. But most of all was the fear of the dark. I dreaded each time the sun would set. This crippling fear carried over into my adulthood and marriage. The only time I wasn't afraid of the dark was when my ex-husband was home. Sometimes when the anxiety became intense, I ran out of my apartment, drive to the base, then sleep in my car.

Once when my ex was on deployment for a couple of weeks, I was all alone. That first night the Lord told me to turn off all the lights in the apartment and walk through it with no gospel music playing. I remember shaking and crying.

You couldn't tell me I wasn't seeing and hearing things. As I walked through the apartment, the Lord began to tell me who He is and who I am in Him. I began to pray within myself, out loud and spoke in tongues. I recited 2 Timothy 1:7 repeatedly. Suddenly, a perfect peace came over me and I began to laugh, a deep belly laugh. At that moment, the Lord delivered me from the fear of darkness. I no longer sleep with any lights unless I want to. Amen. Praise Jesus. I am no longer bound by the spirit of fear. For whom the Son set free is free indeed (John 8:36).

Golden Nuggets

Fear is a prison that prevents tomorrow.

Fear can keep you stuck just like quicksand. It buries you alive with all your dreams unfulfilled.

Fear cancels hope.

Fear closes the door on opportunity.

Success is fearless.

Fear keeps you on the outskirts but faith and truth causes you to enter the gates and go beyond the veil.

Fear keeps you from making decisions.

Procrastination is fear frozen in place.

Fear is progress frozen in time and in place.

Want to overcome faith? Just do it anyway.

Fear is a death sentence. No life, joy, and peace.

Fear is likened to the need to breathe, but you're too afraid to do it, so you don't, and die.

Fear is a stronghold that invites others (spirits) in to have a house party.

Fear keeps you stuck in your past to be tormented by the ghost of your former.

Fear hinders intimacy with GOD.

Fear wrecks and destroys relationships.

Cast all your fears or anxieties to Jesus. He's more than able to handle it.

Fear is a cancer that kills, steals and destroys faith, purpose and destiny.

Fear is like a weed that spreads in your lawn, only to take the life of the good grass.

Uproot fear and soar like an eagle in God.

Fear is a deceiver. It will trick you into believing the lie and not the truth of who God is.

Fear makes things appear bigger than they really are.

Fear will cause you to compromise your integrity.

Fear is paralysis and faith renewed is rehabilitation.

Fear is stagnant waters that don't move and become a breeding ground for mosquitos. Mosquitos that bite and suck your blood, or the life out of you.

Fear doesn't travel alone.

≈

Fear is an open house to more spirits, more fears.

No fear. Go get your life.

CHAPTER 4

God's Promises

Wait[3] (verb)

To remain in place or position without moving or changing. To anticipate or expect someone or something.

Synonyms:

Still, quiet, hope, delay.

---

3. Merriam-Webster.com Dictionary, s.v. "wait," accessed September 9, 2020, https://www.merriam-webster.com/dictionary/wait.

Scripture:

Isaiah 40:31 says, "But they that wait upon the Lord shall renew their strength; they shall mount up with wings as eagles, they shall run, and not be weary; and they shall walk, and not faint."

Learning to be still and waiting on GOD was learned with the help of the Holy Ghost. Always being busy was a silencer for my pain. But one day, I heard a word, "Wait and learn of me my daughter." Waking up and being still before my maker, I basked in the presence of the Lord. It's in Him that my mourning was turned into joy and my ashes was turned into beauty. Oh, the countless times I cried out for Jesus to make sense of my pain and to dry my weeping eyes. The Lord would say, "It's not in vain." For God makes all things beautiful in His time. Today I see snippets of it all and I say thank you Jesus.

Golden Nuggets

It's not in the loud, but it's in the still that I make my thoughts known.

A clear mind makes way for revelation.

To be quiet is to be at peace with our creator.

Quietness is golden.

Many fear the quiet and just like Martha. They are Busy. Be still so I can speak to you.

Stop...Wait...Be Still...Now see me move.

I need you to just stop and be quiet. I want to impart into you. All of me is what I want to give you.

Wait, your spirit is in need of refreshing.

Allow the Holy Ghost to teach you to wait in my presence and how to leave my presence.

Quietness in God births inspiration, creativity, and intimacy.

Wait, it's coming. I am GOD and I cannot lie.

I watch over my words, promises, prophecies, and dreams to perform it. Though it tarries, wait for it. Wait for the manifestation.

Stillness is discipline.

Stillness is a requirement in God's presence.

Waiting in and on the Lord is a precursor to visitation.

In the waiting, you will hear God's silence before you hear His voice.

To wait is to trust and to trust is to believe that God is the Great I AM.

I wait on you Lord. I am not in a hurry because you know what is best for me.

I have need of you Jesus, so I wait.

I wait on you Lord and I dare not get in a hurry.

Waiting is a position of praise. It pleases God.

Waiting is an outward sign of faith. I will not move until my change comes.

Be like Jacob, wait, hold on for your breakthrough.

It is in your presence Lord that I can be me.

Got God's presence?

Need a clue? Get in the presence of God.

Seek me and you will find what you're looking for.

Seeking God, answers questions.

I am waiting because I trust Jesus.

Will you wait or will you abort your purpose and destiny?

Seek Jesus. He is the answer.

It is in the waiting that character is refined.

To wait is an art form that speaks volumes.

To wait is to be full-term and not to wait is being born prematurely, not fully developed, or processed.

Waiting is a killer of the flesh.

To wait is like a grain of corn falling into the ground and dying. Only to produce, bringing forth fruit. So wait, die to self and be fruitful.

CHAPTER 5

Single[4] (adjective)

Consisting of a separate unique whole, individual. Exclusive, attentive, unbroken, undivided.

Synonyms:

Free, unattached, focused, unique.

Scripture:

---

4. Merriam-Webster.com Dictionary, s.v. "single," accessed September 9, 2020, https://www.merriam-webster.com/dictionary/single.

1 Corinthians 7:32-35 says, "But I would have you without carefulness. He that is unmarried careth for the things that belong to the Lord, how he may please the Lord: But he that is married careth for the things that are of the world, how he may please his wife. There is a difference also between a wife and a virgin. The unmarried woman careth for the things of the Lord, that she may be holy both in body and in spirit: but she that is married careth for the things of the world, how she may please her husband. And this I speak for your own profit: not that I may cast a snare upon you, but for that which is comely, and that you may attend upon the Lord without distraction."

As a young divorced woman, I felt like a failure and forsaken because I failed once again. Condemnation made me feel like I was not enough and unlovable. It was in my singleness that the Lord dealt with all of me. It was not about what he or she did or didn't do. The emphasis was me, Sandra. Every relationship/soul tie I had outside of marriage left pieces of me in ruins. So, by the time I got married, I was a hot mess. I was broken and so wounded and therefore was incapable of being or becoming one with another. I tried so many times to find fulfillment in things and in relationships. One-time Jesus told me, "Sandra, I made you and you are a vase, my vessel and no one can fulfill you but me." I yielded, surrendered and became clay in His hands. He put me back together again. I know what it is to be single in Jesus. I remember when I was the Singles minister at my church. My message to the singles was that "You haven't lived till you learned to be single in Jesus."

Golden Nuggets

Single and content in Jesus.

I am single in Jesus and I have God's standards.

Single and focused.

Single with no distractions.

Single. What's next? I have work to do for the Lord.

Single and deadly because I'm focused.

I'm not frigid. I choose Holiness.

I will not be found with any oil in my lamp. I'm single and available to you Lord.

Single and lost in ministry.

Ruth got lost, busy gleaning (busy in ministry) and Boaz found her.

Get lost in Jesus so you can be found.

Single + Jesus = One with Jesus.

Singleness of the heart is to be happy with Jesus.

Singleness of the heart positions you to be blessed by God because He knows you will not love the blessing more than the Blesser.

Singles are the yes men and yes women to the Body of Christ.

Single and driven with purpose.

Single and I am available Lord, take my life and do as you please.

It's all about you Jesus and I seek to please you.

Lord, make me a container of your glory, fill me up and may I spill out and smell like you.

I am a kingdom builder and Jesus is my architect.

Distractions are not my portion.

Single and full of vision.

Single and not alone.

Singleness in God is a sacrifice of Praise.

I'm betrothed to Jesus Christ.

Single and never duplicated. I'm unique.

Singleness is a gift of God.

Singleness of the heart is a deadly weapon. I am a walking and talking loaded gun in Jesus.

Single and totally committed to you Lord. I'm sold out.

Single and seeking to be like Jesus.

Watch out Satan!! I'm single and focused.

Single and consecrated, set aside by Jesus.

Single and holy.

Single and at peace because I know who I am in Christ.

You cannot love God and be married to the world and its systems.

Choose this day whom you will serve Jesus or Satan.

CHAPTER 6

Overcoming Challenges of the Heart

Heart[5] (noun)

The emotional center of a person's thoughts, especially love or compassion. The central or innermost part of something.

---

5. Merriam-Webster.com Dictionary, s.v. "heart," accessed September 9, 2020, https://www.merriam-webster.com/dictionary/heart.

Synonyms:

Soul, mind, passion, and will.

Scriptures:

Matthew 5:8 says, "Blessed are the pure in heart: for they shall see GOD."

Proverbs 4:23 says, "Keep thy heart with all diligence; for out of it are the issues of life."

Holiness[6] (verb)

Dedicated, consecrated, to GOD or a religious purpose, sacred.

Synonyms:

Sanctified, blessed, dedicated, goodness, pure.

Scriptures:

---

6. Merriam-Webster.com Dictionary, s.v. "holiness," accessed September 9, 2020, https://www.merriam-webster.com/dictionary/holiness.

Hebrews 12:14 says, "Follow peace with all men, and holiness; without which no man shall see GOD."

1 Peter 1:15-16 says, "But as he which hath called you is holy, so be ye holy in all manner of conversation; Because it is written, Be ye holy; for I am holy."

Prayer[7] (noun)

A solemn request or expression of thanks to a deity or object of worship.

Synonyms:

Petition, plead, to make known in humility.

Scripture:

Philippians 4:6 says, "Be careful for nothing, but in everything by prayer and supplication with thanksgiving let your request be known unto God."

---

7. Merriam-Webster.com Dictionary, s.v. "prayer," accessed September 9, 2020, https://www.merriam-webster.com/dictionary/prayer.

In retrospect, when I came to Christ, my heart was hard, angry, and full of vengeance. Since there was a deep-rooted hatred for people and myself, I held on to grudges. I remember not speaking to two family members for 7-8 years. They simply did not exist to me. Shortly after becoming a Christian, I was convicted. I called them, repented for my behavior, then asked them to forgive me. I told them that I loved them, which was the beginning process of my heart being changed. I must be honest. It wasn't easy in myself. The issues of my heart affected every aspect of my life. It was difficult for me to receive and give love. I lived by the three strikes you're out rule.

A lot of my anger was directed towards men. Unfortunately, my spiritual brothers were at the receiving end of my wrath. However, I knew I didn't want to be like this, for I desired healthy relationships. I wanted a compassionate heart more than anything. Ezekiel 36:26 was the scripture I prayed and confessed. God, take away my stony heart and give me a new heart and a new spirit. I'm so thankful that the Lord hears the prayers of the righteous. Jesus did it! One Sunday morning at church, the spirit of the Lord was in the house and His glory filled the temple. I began to feel a heat in my chest. I literally saw the hand of God take out what looked like a piece of concrete with chains wrapped around it, which was my heart. Then I saw a hand with a bright red heart that was pulsating, and I could hear the heartbeat, "LUB DUB LUB DUB." This heart was put in my chest. While this occurred, I was speechless. Jesus performed open-heart surgery on me, and I didn't feel the same. I felt so light while LOVE and COMPASSION overwhelmed me. I hugged every brother and told them I loved them. My life was never the same. Thank You, Jesus, for fixing my heart.

Golden Nuggets

Holiness is the path that opens the door for Jesus to habituate.

Holiness is the key that gives you access to the visitation of God.

A pure heart is a guarantee that you'll see God.

A pure heart is an entrance to God's presence.

Give God your heart and you will be transformed.

The Holy Ghost is the gatekeeper of the heart.

The heart only speaks what's in it.

Don't let your heart tell on you. Get it right.

The heart will tell on you every time. For out of the abundance of the heart, does it speak.

A person's whose speech is pure is a person that's been filtered by the Holy Ghost.

Let God purify your heart and everything else will line up.

Sanctification is the filtration system of the Holy Ghost.

The Holy Ghost is a screen. If you yield to Him, He will discern and remove the impurities of your heart.

The Holy Ghost will make you clean.

Give God your heart and be forever changed.

Nations, countries, and communities can be changed when the heart of the people is changed by God.

The heart is likened to a sponge. Be careful of what you absorb.

Repentance squeezes out the impurities of the heart.

Pray for the heart of America that she would let go of her idols.

A new heart and a new song I will give you.

Give me a freewill offering of your heart and watch me give you a heart of gold.

To be holy and consecrated, one must be careful of the company you keep. Let not your good be evil spoken of.

Want a compassionate heart? Then pray for your enemies. Your heart will be changed. It will melt with my love and the love of Christ.

I'm a worshipper of Christ because He has melted my heart. I bleed tears of repentance and I cry the praise of Jesus.

Acknowledgement, confession and repentance are the patterns of a whole heart.

A pure heart is a heart without undercurrents, or hidden agendas.

To be holy, set apart, and consecrated, one must be careful of the company you keep. Let not your good be evil spoken of.

Praying people is a fighting people.

Pray or be prey.

Feeling weak? Then pray.

Prayer is a heart transformer.

Pray for your enemies' vice getting even.

Stop looking at the person and pray for the spirit that is in operation.

A praying spirit gives you a Christ perspective.

The key to not walking in offense is to pray and ask God to forgive them, for they know not what they do.

Prayer gives you the staying power to endure like a good soldier of Jesus Christ.

A tongue talking, interceding saint is the enemy most wanted.

Prayer is not a selection, but it is a requirement of every child of God.

CHAPTER 7

God's Comfort

Live[8] (verb)

To remain alive, occupy, dwell, stay.

Synonyms:

Reside, be settled, experience, have an exciting or fulfilling life.

---

8. Merriam-Webster.com Dictionary, s.v. "live," accessed September 9, 2020, https://www.merriam-webster.com/dictionary/live.

Life[9] (noun/adjective)

The capacity for growth, reproduction, functional activity.

Synonyms:

Existence, state, positioning, lifestyle, soul.

Scriptures:

John 10:10 says, "The thief cometh not, but for to steal, and to kill, and to destroy. I am come that they might have life and that more abundantly".

John 3:16 says, "For God so loved the world, that he gave his only begotten Son, that whosoever believeth in him should not perish, but have everlasting life."

Everyone has issues and boy, did I have them. They were the ghost of my past, which kept me locked down and I was unable to live life freely. I was the caged bird that couldn't sing because

---
9. Merriam-Webster.com Dictionary, s.v. "life," accessed September 9, 2020, https://www.merriam-webster.com/dictionary/life.

I was bound. I learned to cast all my cares upon Him. I presented all my hurts and issues as gifts, wrapped up in boxes with pretty bows and laid them at His feet. I told Jesus that I couldn't carry them anymore because I wanted to live life spontaneously. I also told the Lord that I trusted Him with my life.

Golden Nuggets

Live life without tomorrows, yesterdays or I should 'ofs.' Live life now.

Live life as if today is your last day.

Life is but a vapor. Live and flourish now.

Live life without regrets or missed opportunities. Once it passes it's gone.

Only God can redeem time.

The greatest peace is knowing who you are in God.

Knowing your purpose is the first step to succeeding in life.

When you know your identity in Christ, nothing in life will move you.

To be focused is to know where you're going because you have vision.

Live life today and make memories that'll last a lifetime.

Don't be content with just existing. Pursue life and flourish in it. You can be like a cedar tree abiding in my courtyard.

Every day you live is a memory. So make the most of your todays.

Life's memories are pictures that pass from one generation to another.

Jesus is the chief corner stone, carpenter, and the creator of everything. Trust him with your life.

A moment in time is like a drip of water. Once it drips, you can never get it back. It's gone.

Don't live life on the sidelines. Get involved, engage, and experience it.

Go get your life.

Want inspiration for living? Take a drive or walk thru a cemetery. There lies so many unfulfilled dreams, visions, regrets and should 'ofs.'

Life is worth living in Christ.

A bored Christian is a one that's not abiding in Christ.

Stay connected to Jesus and live your best life.

Stay connected to the vine and live your best life. Jesus came that we have life and life more abundantly.

To have a peace of mind and heart, is living a blessed life.

My life, seasons, and destiny are in your hands.

You can trust the Father with your life, so relax and exhale. He got you.

CHAPTER 8

The Result (Process, Promotion, Testimony and Destiny)

Process [10](noun)

A series of changes that occur naturally in the growth process. A series of actions or steps taken in order to achieve an end.

---
10. Merriam-Webster.com Dictionary, s.v. "process," accessed September 9, 2020, https://www.merriam-webster.com/dictionary/process.

Synonyms:

Procedures, tests, exercises, tasks.

Promotion[11] (noun)

The act of raising to a higher position or rank.

Synonyms:

Elevate, higher position, raise, advance.

Testimony[12] (noun)

Evidence or proof provided by the existence or appearance of something.

Synonyms:

Witness, statement, proof, manifestation.

Destiny[13] (noun)

---

11. Merriam-Webster.com Dictionary, s.v. "promotion," accessed September 9, 2020, https://www.merriam-webster.com/dictionary/promotion.
12. Merriam-Webster.com Dictionary, s.v. "testimony," accessed September 9, 2020, https://www.merriam-webster.com/dictionary/testimony.
13 Merriam-Webster.com Dictionary, s.v. "destiny," accessed September 9,

The event that will necessarily happen to a person or thing in the future.

Synonyms:

Due, future, portion, predestination.

***Strong's14 5056**

Toll, an end, aim, purpose, the principal end, unfolding.

Scriptures:

Philippians 1:6 says, "Being confident of this very thing, that he which begun a good work in you will perform it until the day of Jesus Christ."

Psalms 75:6 says, "Promotion cometh neither from the east, nor from the west, nor from the south. But GOD is the judge; he putteth down one, and setteth up another."

2020, https://www.merriam-webster.com/dictionary/destiny

Revelation 12:11 says, "And they overcame him by the blood of the lamb and by the word of their testimony; and they loved not their lives unto death."

Jeremiah 29:11 says, "For I know the thoughts that I think toward you, saith the Lord, thoughts of peace, and not evil, to give you an expected end."

I had to learn that it's not wise to compare myself or my walk in Christ with others, for in doing so, I became discouraged, wondering why and what's wrong with me? Repeatedly I was told that God was going to take me through a long process but in the end, the prophetic, healing and deliverance ministry would be birthed. So many times, I wanted to abort because the pain was so deep and raw. I was misunderstood, judged and treated like an afterthought. God kept telling me that everything I went through wasn't in vain and that one day it will all make sense. Jesus promised me that my pain would be turned into power and my weeping will be turned into joy. I held on with a tight grip to Jesus while allowing myself to be processed and healed. The eyes of my understanding have been opened. Now I see and walking in my destiny.

Golden Nuggets

Nothing is wasted in God.

Don't be ashamed of your testimony.

Don't sit on your testimony. Someone needs to hear your story and be set free.

Your testimony is your anointed autobiography that will help others make it through.

I'm so glad I made it over. I got a testimony!

When you can tell your story, you have overcome because of the blood of the lamb.

Tried and Tested. I'm an Overcomer!

I shall come forth as gold because I was able to bear the heat of my process and testing.

Your testimony cost you, so tell it!

Testify, tell it and silence the devil.

I promise I'm going to use your story for my glory.

No one can tell your story or testimony because it's anointed with your pain and tears.

Do you want a testimony? Can you stand to be tested?

As a Christian, you will and shall have trails, but it's how you handled them that matters.

How you handle opposition is an indicator of one's character.

Opposition handled properly is a precursor to maturity.

Test and trails overcame is a testament of how you made it.

I'm pressed for greatness.

True character is revealed during the times of trails.

Pass the test and graduate into your promise.

Your pressing, testing hour produces the best you.

I'm not a survivor, but I'm an overcomer because Jesus has healed my wounds.

I'm healed because my wounds have become scars.

Stand and testify. You have been healed, delivered, and restored. You're free.

Your testimony is significant, even the crumbs. Yes, those things you call ugly and the unmentionable.

Without my pain, trials, etc., I wouldn't be who I am today. So Lord, I thank you for my story and my testimony.

Beauty for your ashes is when you can tell your story and see the beauty of how it all works together for the good and for saving of lives.

I am going to use all the crumbs of your life. Nothing is wasted in God.

No Shame. Tell It. You're Free.

I have a testimony. I am free in Jesus. My past no longer torments me.

Tell your story and be set free from the shadows of your past.

How you handle frustrations determines your level of promotion.

You don't have to brown nose or kiss up to man. Promotion comes from God.

The opinion of man ought not phase you. If God is pleased, then that's all that matters.

When God says it's time, no devil in hell can stop it.

Adversity endured in integrity will take you to your next level in God.

Separate from all that hinders you, so that God can elevate you.

Sometimes to go higher in God, you got to let go of some people, places and things.

You can't take everybody with you because it's not for them.

Lighten the load and cross over into your destiny.

In transitioning into your destiny, you'll discover who's really for you and who's not.

When you know who you are, you will walk in what God said. You'll find that people will become uncomfortable or insecure. They will try to make you feel or deflect that you're not right, hearing correctly or off point. Pray for their insecurities and continue to walk in what God said.

Promotion is in God's timing and not man's. When it's your time and season, it's because God ordained it to be.

A person of integrity is a person with Godly character.

God promoted me. If you have a problem with it, see God.

God watches over His word. Every prophecy, dream, and vision concerning you will be manifested at His set time.

God makes all things beautiful in His time. Complete the process.

Destiny killers are like vampires. They'll suck the life out of you (your dreams, vision and purpose).

Hanging with vampires will make you like the living dead.

Avoid certain places because every place isn't for you, especially when crossing over into your destiny or promise land.

Pray for God to connect you with your destiny helpers and to discern when you meet them.

People of vision are always moving and people without vision are like a shapeless mass; a mass without definition, clarity or purpose. They are in a state of nothingness.

A person that watches a lot of TV has no vision, purpose, and future.

Check your company and life. Make the necessary adjustments.

A negative person is like a cement block. It will weigh you down spiritually.

I don't have time for pettiness. I'm destiny bound.

Hanging with doers of the Word of God provokes inspiration.

Prophetic people are the matches, the sparks of every fire (dream, vision, or destiny).

Watching long hours of TV is waving bye to your destiny and purpose. Watch as it passes you by.

To be purpose driven is destiny in movement.

Keep Moving = Walking in Destiny.

Believe my prophets and your life will be established and prosperous. Walk in it and put it into action.

Timing is everything. Processed leads to being promoted by God so destiny can be fulfilled.

Don't mistake giftings and anointing for character. Godly character is staying true, or the same when the heat is on.

Giftings and anointing may open doors, but its integrity that keeps the doors open.

Your gift may elevate you, but its integrity that'll take you far and give you longevity in ministry.

Show me a person of integrity and I'll say his word is his bond.

Pursue unshakeable integrity.

You were created for this. Now is the time.

You were created for this moment in God.

I praise God like I do because I know what it took to be here.

Yahweh knows me. He was there all the time.

Remember Lot's wife and don't look back. Walk forward into your future and destiny.

Don't get stuck in your past. Keep moving. Allow God to process you.

To be processed is to ensure your warranty in Christ won't expire.

To be processed is to be tested, tried by fire and pasted with Jesus' grace.

We're processed so we won't die in our season. It gives you longevity in Christ.

Whatever you do, don't stop. You're so close to the end and your destiny.

Onward March!! Keep Moving. Do something.

Let it go and leave it. Don't look back. For you weren't created to look backwards but forward.

New sound. New revelation. It's a new season.

Listen to the sound of God and pay attention.

With every new move, there's a sound of God. You'll find instructions and guidance.

Keep Pharaoh (your past) buried.

God will hide your past from you. He'll take the sting away and hide it from your enemies.

Giants are defeated because I see the promised land and I see how it ends. I'm walking in destiny. The end of it all is fulfilled.

About The Author

Sandra L. Ross is a minister, teacher, worshipper, and poet. Sandra has served in multiple areas in ministry, but her greatest love is for the brokenhearted and those bound by pain from their past. Sandra is a true witness of the wonder working power of God in her life. Sandra experienced the ugliness of abuse and all it entails. She lived life as a victim. But one day, she heard a word, "It's Not in Vain." With this new perspective, her life was never the same. No longer walking in shame, her mourning was turned into dancing, and she was given beauty for her ashes. No longer living her life as a victim, Sandra is a survivor because the wounds did not kill her but birthed in her a passion to see people released from the prisons of their pain and to be made whole.

References

1. Merriam-Webster.com Dictionary, s.v. "faith," accessed September 9, 2020, https://www.merriam-webster.com/dictionary/faith.

2. Merriam-Webster.com Dictionary, s.v. "fear," accessed September 9, 2020, https://www.merriam-webster.com/dictionary/fear.

3. Merriam-Webster.com Dictionary, s.v. "wait," accessed September 9, 2020, https://www.merriam-webster.com/dictionary/wait.

4. Merriam-Webster.com Dictionary, s.v. "single," accessed September 9, 2020, https://www.merriam-webster.com/dictionary/single.

5. Merriam-Webster.com Dictionary, s.v. "heart," accessed September 9, 2020, https://www.merriam-webster.com/dictionary/heart.

6. Merriam-Webster.com Dictionary, s.v. "holiness," accessed September 9, 2020, https://www.merriam-webster.com/dictionary/holiness.

7. Merriam-Webster.com Dictionary, s.v. "prayer," accessed September 9, 2020, https://www.merriam-webster.com/dictionary/prayer.

8. Merriam-Webster.com Dictionary, s.v. "live," accessed September 9, 2020, https://www.merriam-webster.com/dictionary/live.

9. Merriam-Webster.com Dictionary, s.v. "life," accessed September 9, 2020, https://www.merriam-webster.com/dictionary/life.

10. Merriam-Webster.com Dictionary, s.v. "process," accessed September 9, 2020, https://www.merriam-webster.com/dictionary/process.

11. Merriam-Webster.com Dictionary, s.v. "promotion," accessed September 9, 2020, https://www.merriam-webster.com/dictionary/promotion.

12. Merriam-Webster.com Dictionary, s.v. "testimony," accessed September 9, 2020, https://www.merriam-webster.com/dictionary/testimony.

13. Merriam-Webster.com Dictionary, s.v. "destiny," accessed September 9, 2020, https://www.merriam-webster.com/dictionary/destiny.

14. "G5056 - telos - Strong's Greek Lexicon (KJV)." Blue Letter Bible. Accessed 9 Sep, 2020. https://www.blueletterbible.org//lang/lexicon/lexicon.cfm?Strongs=g5056&t=kjv

Index

A

abundance, 36
access, 35
activated, 6, 7, 10
agendas, 38
alive, 14, 40
anger, 34
animal, 10
anointed, 50, 51
anticipate, 18
anxiety,, 13
apartment, 6, 13, 14
architect, 28

ashamed, 50
ashes, 19, 53, 62
ATM card, 7

B

beautiful, 5, 19, 55
beauty, 19, 53, 62
believe., 9, 11
blessing, 27
blood, 17, 49, 50

C

California, 5
cancer, 16
catalyst, 10
Challenges, 31
change, 9, 10, 11, 22
character, 23, 51, 52, 55, 57
chest, 35
Christ, 2, 5, 6, 28, 29, 34, 38, 43, 44, 48, 49, 58, 59
Christian, 2, 3, 34, 44, 51
coins, 2
Comfort, 40

compassion, 31
confession, 38
confidence, 4, 5
consecrated, 29, 32, 38
courage, 13
creativity, 20
creator, 20, 42
crying, 13

D

danger, 12
deceiver, 16
dedicated, 32
Dedicated, 32
destiny, 16, 22, 45, 47, 50, 54, 56, 57, 58, 59, 60
Destiny, 46, 47, 55, 57
destroys, 16
discern, 37, 56
distractions, 26
divorced, 25
door, 6, 14, 35
dread, 13
Dreaming, 7
dreams, 14, 21, 44, 55
dwell, 40

E

eagle, 16
emotion, 12
emotional, 31
encouragement, 3
enemies, 38, 59
engage, 44
evil, 38, 49
expectation, 12

F

failure, 25
faith, 2, 3, 4, 5, 6, 7, 8, 9, 10, 11, 15, 16, 22
Favor, 7
fear, 2, 3, 12, 13, 14, 15, 16, 17, 20
Fear, 12, 14, 15, 16, 17
fearless, 15
flood flash, 2
flourish, 41, 42
forsaken, 25
fruitful, 23
frustrations, 53
future, 48, 56, 58

G

gatekeeper, 36
gates, 15
generation, 43
Giftings, 57
glory, 28, 35, 51
God, 2, 4, 5, 6, 7, 8, 9, 10, 11, 13, 16, 18, 19, 20, 21, 22, 26, 27, 28, 29, 33, 34, 35, 36, 37, 40, 41, 42, 49, 50, 53, 54, 55, 56, 57, 58, 59, 61
GOD, 9, 10, 15, 19, 21, 32, 33, 48
gold, 37, 50
golden coins, 2
golden nuggets, 2, 3
growth, 41, 46

H

happy, 27
heart, 2, 27, 29, 31, 32, 34, 35, 36, 37, 38, 44
Heart, 31
heart issues, 2
heavens, 1
help, 2, 19, 50
holiness, 32, 33
Holiness, 27, 32, 35

Holy Ghost, 3, 19, 20, 36, 37
hope, 2, 14, 18
humility, 33

I

idle., 7
idols, 37
impossible., 8
impurities, 37
insects., 10
insecurities, 54
inspiration, 20, 44, 56
integrity., 16, 58
intimacy, 13, 15, 20

J

Jesus, 2, 3, 14, 16, 19, 21, 22, 26, 27, 28, 29, 30, 34, 35, 38, 42, 43, 44, 48, 49, 52, 53, 59
Jesus., 3, 14, 16, 19, 22, 26, 27, 29, 38, 53
joy, 15, 19, 49

K

kills, 16

kingdom builder, 28

L

lamp, 27
laugh, 14
lie, 16, 21
life, 15, 16, 17, 28, 32, 34, 35, 40, 41, 42, 43, 44, 45, 53, 55, 56, 57, 61, 62
lifestyle, 40
Lord, 1, 2, 5, 6, 13, 14, 19, 21, 22, 25, 27, 28, 29, 34, 35, 42, 49, 52
love, 3, 13, 27, 29, 31, 34, 38, 61

M

manifestation, 21, 47
marriage, 13, 25
memory, 43
mercy, 3
mind, 20
minister, 3, 26, 61
ministry, 27, 49, 58, 61
miracle, 6, 10
monarch butterflies, 5
money, 2

mountains, 8
mourning, 19, 61
muscle, 9

N

newspaper, 5

O

oil, 27
opposition, 51
overcome, 15, 50
Overcoming, 31
overwhelmed, 35

P

pain, 19, 49, 51, 52, 61, 62
paralysis., 8
past, 15, 41, 53, 58, 59, 61
peace, 14, 15, 20, 29, 33, 42, 44, 49
perish, 41
plant, 10
position, 18, 22, 47
pray, 3, 14, 38

presence, 19, 20, 21, 22, 36
process, 34, 46, 49, 50, 55, 58
Process, 46
Procrastination, 15
Promises, 18
promises., 3
Promotion, 46, 47, 48, 53, 55
prophecies, 21
prophetic, 49
provision., 10
pure, 32, 36, 38
purpose, 16, 22, 28, 32, 43, 48, 55, 56, 57
Pursue, 43, 58

Q

quicksand, 14
quiet, 18, 20

R

raining, 2
regrets, 42, 44
rehabilitation, 16
relationships, 13, 16, 26, 34
repentance, 38

revelation, 20, 59
righteous, 34

S

sacrifice, 28
Sanctified, 32
savings account, 7
Scripture, 5, 13, 19, 24, 33
season, 2, 55, 59
shaking, 11, 13
sick, 8
Single, 24, 26, 27, 28, 29
soar, 16
Son, 14, 41
song, 37
Soul, 32
sound mind, 13
spirits, 15, 17
stagnant, 17
steals, 16
Still, 18, 20
Stillness, 21
strength, 3, 19
stronghold, 15
Success, 15

sun, 1
survivor, 52, 62

T

teacher, 61
testimony, 47, 49, 50, 51, 52, 53
Testimony, 46, 47
time, 5, 13, 15, 19, 25, 26, 36, 42, 44, 53, 55, 56, 58
tongues, 14
transformed, 36
treasures, 3
trust, 3, 4, 7, 10, 21, 22, 45
Trust, 5, 43
truth, 15, 16
TV, 56, 57

U

Unbelief, 8
unexpected, 8
unexplainable, 8
unique, 24, 29

V

vengeance, 34
victim, 61, 62
vision, 1, 28, 43, 55, 56, 57
visitation, 21, 35
visitation., 21

W

wait, 18, 19, 20, 21, 22, 23
warranty, 57
wave of water, 1
weary, 19
weeping, 19, 49
wife, 25, 58
wind, 6
windowpane, 1
wisdom, 2
Wisdom, 2
witness, 61
Words, 9, 11
worship, 33